joanne burns | brush

New Poems

GIRAMONDO POETS

joanne burns | brush

First published 2014
from the Writing & Society Research Centre
at the University of Western Sydney
by the Giramondo Publishing Company
PO Box 752 Artarmon NSW 1570 Australia
www.giramondopublishing.com

Designed by Harry Williamson
Typeset by Andrew Davies
in 10/16.5 pt Baskerville

Printed and bound by Ligare
Distributed in Australia by NewSouth Books

National Library of Australia
Cataloguing-in-Publication data:

burns, joanne
brush / joanne burns

978-1-922146-71-7 (pbk)

A821.3

Other books by joanne burns

Snatch
Ratz
Alphabatics
Adrenalin Flicknife
Radio City 2am – with Stefanie Bennett and Ruth K. Fordham
Correspondences – with Pamela Brown
ventriloquy
blowing bubbles in the seventh lane
on a clear day
penelope's knees
aerial photography
people like that
footnotes of a hammock
an illustrated history of dairies
amphora

Acknowledgements

Best American Poems Blog, *Cordite*, *Famous Reporter*, *foam:e*, *four W*, *HEAT*, *Mascara*, *Meanjin*, *Otoliths*, *Overland*, *Perihelion*, *Polari*, *Snorkel*, *Social Alternatives*, *Sun Herald/Red Room Company*, *Age*. *Conversations from the Bottom of the Harbour* and *Harbour City Poems* (Puncher and Wattmann 2009); *Guide to Sydney Beaches* (Meuse Press 2009); *Mud Maps: Australian Women's Experimental Writing*, *Text* online journal 2013; *Notes for the Translators* (ASM Poetry Macau 2012); *Small Wonder* (Spineless Wonders 2012); *The Best Australian Poems* 2008–2013 (Black Inc); *The Turnrow Anthology of Contemporary Australian Poetry* (turnrow books, ULM Press 2014); *Wording the World* (Puncher and Wattmann 2010).

This project has been assisted by the Commonwealth Government through the Australia Council, its arts funding and advisory body.

Contents

bluff

factoidal

does your share portfolio ache
unlock your teeth in the adrenal winds,
the facilitationality of a sea of nomadic desks
doesn't need to be seen to be believed –
flotsam and jetsam are serious navigators
in this expedition of trust, new world
values never as new as invention;
you were born with collateralised genes
zenned up couch pod tycoon
invest in your personal equator
it's neptune or never

corrida

i. business as usual

it's war, the meat pie bonus
staff were arrested offended and
intact that's what you get with
the arms length approach to the
corrida's history although bakers
have more control over their pies
people want to see real chunks;
still the platinum diversification
code means it's not all meat,
ravenous fans have been seen
romancing fish and vegetables
in the hybrid blood spas so surprise
surprise

the jaguar threw a lavish
party on a host of solar panels
i'm a bit nervous doing my
sums in the steel mill foyer
the thought of that green halo
eloping – the window would
only wind down just an inch
stone walls are still a feature
of a head

ii. manifest/er

the surprise decision on the bumpy road
to grammar, a coup in the diary covenant
well received; trapped in its own web the vacant
chair diverse as an emotive phrase restructured
the backyard; and who would have imagined
a bus driver to return like a prodigal sun
from the versailles exploration thesis, the arrival
party at the tower of london was acute and
taciturn – some still believed it was best
to trim the hedges some were tight lipped
about the rosey picture – and this could
wipe out any benefit from the plan to divide
the good from the bad   everyone was happy

though about the 19 billion sound rescue package
the final comment 'we misjudged how quickly
syllables could turn around'   one of the best
sellers was the seamless camisole someone
suddenly declared

iii. tough love

it's the city of optimists
the bulls are roaring
over the leftovers shining
like gift cards there
are pizzas so new the
olives are still on the trees

here are pavements lined
with almonds myth solid
as guides to the holy land
and spiced lamb on tooth picks
to sample while the chefs
get on with cooking the books

and the patient ocean so
energetic in the titanium lobbies
no shortage of people to count

iv. lotional

portafiled in waterproof snaplock plastic
share portfolios will bide their time like
projected family weddings you ought to be
congratulated mums and dads for feathering
your nests intoned the presidential spectacle/s
from a harbour newsroom   it's all ship
shape my friends   leave the old pacific chunder
of tin coins and the crested carpet   that pokie
spew is for the mugs   shares can be your shoreline
or think of it as share farming, as our pastoral
heritage – he ploughed her and she cropped – the pumpkin
will be golden   blue or butternut –

> of course there will be
> complementary seasons   bulls
> and bears   glitches and corrections
> peaks and troughs   but she'll be safe
> as toasted fingers vegemite or anchovette;
> ditch any second thoughts between the calomine
> and chamomile   summer cockroaches will
> eat them up –

v. hilt

the giveaway dead flowers boom:
sprawling mines contemplating
entertainments: the grass pallets
slide: niche profits on a global
dive, you pitch my pool into a
passing buck and i'll ride you into
bank-ruptcy: equine woodchips
pulse for pulse; pretty forecast,
sleep easy on the oil rig bud –
while the internet circum
ambulates the rampant hedge like
a stylebook parent naked in autumn toxic
bones defend the tight rope with choc
aholic con-fidence   have you
recruited yet that winner, jitterbug!

(pas)time

today opens its
stalls   what to wear
a sugar coat or the
raw prawn boardsuit
gambas on the ramblas
shells crush like distressed
property accounts   how
big will the billion dollar
slug grow   swing factor
or slippery dip? the day
brawls   a margin calls,
gamble on, domino domingo

mannafacturing

this week the market
on a roll, more swiss
than sausage and
sweeter than an audit
banks danced with renewed
interest tango fox trot hip
hop [pride of erin?], one
renamed a grandstand, some
dug a little dirt some pondered:
rock bottom really was a long
way down something dreamed up
by cranky old dante; hunger no
longer featherweight the pie discarded
its 'humble' and any link to 'apple
crumble'; crusts rose higher than
flocks of blackbirds rumour more
than a gecko

rehearsal

so many bids were shelved
there was a shortage of walls
for corporate tear squads to
prop themselves against during
the peak of the hoodlum audits
the soy bean and coal chip prices
per bushel forecast so deflatulenced
profits were shocked as they taxied
into austerity drive with its red
tape bunting dividends tripped
over at the pedestrian warning lights
stories retailed like zombies at the
roundabout   next teller please –

bluff

i. equity

bring a plate to the global
table brands are set
to translate into something
more than sulkiness tim
tams will soon greet the aurora
borealis the farm gate is not as
rubbery as it looks   the bone density
dairy carries as much equity as the best
baguette   so don't break the glass of
simple arithmetic, just leave the red
ink out of the jus

ii. pot boiler

surplus romance liquidates
malls god's grim suitors trample
church steps with epic flair buñuel
budgets for a guest list on the verge
of narcoleptic square   is origami
better to snack upon than salvers of
paper balls, well scrunched, with or
without a butler   can charm afford
the discretions of a shell investment

any longer   leaks stench the marketplace
like crabs in boiler rooms   eyes scratch
towards prayer or rupture

iii. write down

take a more conciliatory tone
the bird poo boutique the preferred
vehicle – $5.20 for a cup of coffee
on the kerb another fund manager
backlash, and the gravy train's provided
more splash back than a rogue cooktop,
ruptured cufflinks in the trash compactor;
i saw sourpuss off to voucher island in a
patchwork suit eating canary pie –

iv. fancy

bankers danced the zumba junta
in the constitutional ballroom just
a bit of festive fancy dress like a
tv mockumentary on a bitter winter's
night the pink batt cocktails kept them
warm enough; some escorted current
spouses others escorted escorts there was

a mix up when pecuniary interests were
introduced to love investments, just by chance;
certain guests rang promptly for their drivers, others
rang up potential losses; there was a moment when
the floorboards shifted like a listing, like a tower of
mini pizzas whose anchovies shone like bullets; then
the dollar suddenly shot up reaching the peak of the
continental drapes

chain

a tranche of fresh
air ~ a perfect sail's
pitch for the aspiring
billionaire depleted by
a projected avalanche of
cornflakes and ketchup
debt – the purchase of
a post office chain a
mere distraction for
a dedicated nostagia
gene, tongue licking
good only for a moment
between the envelope and
greeting card display –
but AAA rated air it could
revive those pores
like a yacht in a sunset
clause

in the mood

foyeristic

the email said the meaning was in the second room. she was sure of this. she stood in the foyer of the building. a circular space from which five or six corridors radiated. there was no one at the inquiry desk. brainzak tunes pulsed from tiny lights rosed into the ceiling.

at a quick glance it seemed to her that none of the rooms were numbered. she tried to open the second door in each corridor but every one was locked and no one responded to her knock. she would have to try all of the sixty doors to locate the meaning. and she did. without success. maybe she needed to clean her glasses. or maybe she needed to close her eyes. she tried the second option and walked towards the nearest corridor until she came to the door that felt right. when she opened her eyes the door suddenly fell backwards to reveal a wall sized screen image of a shipwrecked city behind a sign advising 'meeting this way'. ithaca was rather disappointed at the absence of meaning but glad she could remember how to swim.

there's always something falling into one of my eyes. usually the left one. dandruff flakes dropping in for a visit from an eyebrow's foliage. from in between the layers of the canopy. dropping down for some hydration. irritants arriving uninvited. hairs, invisible mites that catch the eye off guard. nothing with the prestige of an icarus. no deep aegean blue or brueghel's green in my ocular curves.

&&&

this eye turns red as if a fierce little theatre has taken possession. red as an avenging god or demon. the chemist girl gasps against the diorama of the make up display. well, i'm not going to casualty. it's an allergic reaction to particles of paint scraped from the window ledge. a small flask of drops will be my exorcist.

&&&

last year i had my first flash and floater moment in my right eye. google was chockablock with explanatory websites. flash and floater – not quite the same as surf and turf. the flash came first as i was having a post-shower epiphany about the prominence of death. i wondered whether all those heritage listed visionaries and mystics simply were victims of retinal mistranslation – something a visit to an eye hospital or an optometrist might have fixed. how dull the fact of the retina being affected by the hardening of the eye's vitreous jelly, compared with the aura of divine revelation.

this tiny floater i've grown used to. my own little arachne. not a regular visitor, but a modest soothsayer and spy. i can't feed it peas but it seems to thrive on migratory dandruff and morsels from the air.

&&&

red veins of an eyeball. perhaps ship routes on a globe or life tracks that need clarification. do not be deterred by their colour. is danger so simple. forget the chiromancer of the palm. become a vasculamancer.

i see you now with your bloodshot eyes standing in the doorway holding a raw egg in a clear glass. the yolk so like a bright fruit suspended in the clear albumen. this was your hangover cure. i believed you. then. the hangovers stopped. the veins in your eyes displayed potential.

&&&

p.s. in nineteen sixty eight i saw a production of 'king lear' at the wagga drama theatre. during the scene where gloucester's eyes were gouged out warwick and i, sitting in the second row, rolled jaffas on the floor.

literate

here. hair floats down towards the floor in a morning's sunlight. time for a moment, like a surprise cadence stroking the throat.

white hairs that have stored a life. lives. frail akashic records. their descent to the hardness of floor boards will filch their timbres. flows and whisps of thought stranded. obliterated. do not underestimate diana and the growling hunger of her vacuum cleaner hounds.

the more you brush the more they fall. is there a stubborn beauty to be observed. in this eloquent decline.

thesaur

know it. that word *treasure*. do you. what do you recognise.

there is a blankness in the muddled room. the lethargic pause of eyes. pallor of their lids. a tolerance of boredom.

treasure. have you thought of it since the covers of juvenile story books snapped it shut.

a word for the suasoriae of lottery lexicons. or the sentimentality of nations. a national treasure. let's have a party of congratulatory tea cosies.

treasure. how might you treasure it. the shift from noun to verb impels.

let its *z* waft through your remaining teeth like a soft zephyr. that halcyonic darkness ahead. it won't cost you a cent.

easy

when you fall you sprawl on the pavement like a virgin swimmer. you lie there stretching for your glasses that have skidded out of reach.

you are yourself. you clamber up. vertical and mobile. your best move. the blood runs down your leg. you cross the road. you rise to the occasion.

a child falls into a wall. a school game. a rush of legs and hands pushing to be first. to touch the bricks. an urgency for home. eyebrow flesh splits open. a little needlework ahead. glasses snap and crackle.

how many falls to go. it is an awkward thing to count. to calculate.

a boy falls from the top of a city tower. a tall boy carrying a note in his pocket insisting god had given him permission to jump. you recollect him walking towards you from the back of the room to ask the meaning of 'vernacular'. you had been impressed.

falling is a kind of vernacular.

dust falls, dates fall, love falls.

when you fall you sometimes dream it is forever.
easy as the weather.

in the mood

i.–x. a mood in progress

i.

on the shelf a ball of pale string never unrolled in a venture an adventure sitting tight and neat as the day of its purchase. can this string unwind and travel forth like the trail of a cautious pilgrim or sleuth attached to home base just in case. it would become such a tangle to wind back to its original shape. would it be worth it. this intrusion on its beauty. its pristinity. would the shelf want it. covered in the muck of the world. would you.

ii.

a will sat near the window under a paper weight. it had sat there so long it had faded in the light. it had lived much longer than it had expected in those distant days when it had been drawn up. it longed for a light wind to lift it. to give it the will and muscle of a weight lifter. the paper weight was so heavy the will sometimes struggled for breath through its dusty skin. sometimes when the sun burnt through the glass of the window it prayed for its own execution.

iii.

the mood lighting knew it was an anachronism. who wanted a room illuminated by all that moody business. it had gone the way of water beds. down the drain. there was enough screenglow to authenticate domestic comfort. and a complementary darkness was embraced. after all mood was a pedantic concept. it was preferable to be enhanced by your surroundings. and stay there.

iv.

light spraying through the morning's shutters like a peacock. a restored moment. the memo pad hectic with telephone numbers. emails carp with duty's jingles. these colours streaming through your sparse eyelids. you smell them like a pram.

v.

no writing remaining on the exponential wall. a fertility of keener scribble. marking time. a gala of concern. keeping itself to itself. repetition and all its luxurious nerves. only to be guessed at. glib translation takes it on the chin. hi reader. who are you. scrape that primer off your back. the inside of the wall itches for your chaperoned essays. the sea scrolls behind you like another dead pastry.

vi.

the chimney on the roof. how long since warm smoke from a lounge room fire rose through it. does its eye glare upwards for answers. does it care. does it need to. television aerials cling to it for all their worth. carting trash of the hot world down below. waiting rooms filled with impatience.

vii.

today i praise disposability, diablo of the ecological lexicon. that liberator from poetryscapeology limited. where a simple cup [china clay porcelain] becomes a repository of meaning, enduring the weight of so much memory, so much association, that you cannot lift it to your lips and drink. a one object museum of redolence. you can only admire it from a distance. when you're in the mood, a dozen breaths away, without thirst. people write poems about cups like this. swoon poems. poems that confuse the sentimental with the sacred. here i have a stack of disposable white cups. one drink cups. and then they go into the bin on their journey to lethe's landfill. you squeeze them as you dispense with them. they crackle with light relief. glad to be departing for deep caves of earth. where sleeping cups are let lie. and the tea leaves little stain.

viii.

i feel like writing. on and on i go. so many false starts, repetitions, extra details. the body grows, skin stretches to fit the words. all those abrasive punctuation marks, confusion of meanings, awkward grammars and clamorous syllables. the underworld of language. my head aches with the load. i feel like writing yet i don't look like writing. do i like writing. not likely or i wouldn't be writing this. but what else is there to do when you only have two hands and eyes that have mislaid the world. through the drinking straw i hear the insects swarming.

ix.

it was a small message. too small to write down. its language was unfamiliar to me but i knew what it meant. if that's all i knew i knew that. had known it since my knees hit the floor. had heard it inside the grass. ticking. tenacious. you wouldn't want to write it down. the soil knew how to cut a long story short.

x.

so often we wash away the evidence. *evidence* you might say. evidence of ourselves. we hang it up to dry. and then we wrap it round our bodies once again. it gathers so much of our absorbent selves we cannot allow it hang too long upon the rack. for the warm intimacies we have shared to turn rank. is this why we are tempted to abandon it wet and crumpled on the tiles. out of fear not squander.

and so we lift the lid of the machine; engage the suds and their cathartic whirls. our towels must be fresh. soft and empty vessels compliant with our ignorant ambiguous desires.

buffet

he said he'd left the cheese roll on the sideboard. made it with his own hands he did. spread the butter. laid out the cheese and pressed the two halves of roll together. like a carpenter not a ploughman. it was his. he did not expect anyone to take it.

something ordinary turns into a dispute. the bland exacting habits of a suited thug in pinterville. his philosopher brother in an almost trenchcoat said he'd eaten it. deliberately. he wanted it. yes. he saw his brother put it on the sideboard earlier in the day. a tenacity hovers in the room.

the empirical cheese roll turns abstract. no blood flows in this fraternal, fastidious episode. all is cold indignation and accomplishment. there is no greek tragedy in which a cheese roll figures. you may thank zeus for that.

brush

a series of day poems

sip

the intonations of the charcoal
ocean from sand to horizon, we sip
on coffee's prophecies as the morning
rises, the detour into gossip by the bay
welcomes the side order of spinach, oysters
levitate like ectoplasm above the menu the omnibus
is swift in its journey to the city that sweeps you into
neon's rhetoric so what is it that you need to see in
such illumination; later you discover that mail addressed
to the garden has been misdelivered, the telephone
consultant gives you a long number: a receipt for your
complaint & you fail to steam the sweet potato long enough

tier

the air is full of rain   the dawn service tiered with umbrellas
faces shine out from the dark upon the screen   i read that
  dad's friend
neville 88 down from tamworth for the march   waits at
  the cenotaph
to talk after the service   war is useless he says   he spoke at
  dad's funeral
in 98   he loves a talk   in and out of hospital   words keep
  him alive
alert   i must remember this   i'll give him a bell next week
  all you have
is what you have   our hard boiled eggs sit in their cups
  without a crack
i sprinkle mine with dulse   a sea vegetable from doctor earth
  a health
food shop   huge trees at the top of ithaca road shine
  emerald green
through the streaky window glass   this wet foliage   fleece of
  giant sheep   the
harbour water worries   war planes invade the sky in a
  shattering display   goodbye
anzac day

dues

the bus driver had run out of tickets
that is senior day excursion ones
by the time i climbed on just after three pm i arrived at the registry
office of births deaths & marriages the automatic doors were being
repaired a flock of people animated the footpath i'm not sure why perhaps
a specialty tour of rites of passage they bore no luggage except their smiles;
inside the counters thick with pamphlets, wads of application forms *i want the one*
for being reborn they're being reprinted an automated voice replied now if i'd
been at the teachers' credit union there'd have been a free drink from the courtesy
fridge to sip on while you did your business there's zilch of that here just a
winding queue i wander limply under sandstone arches & through the fumes of
moody traffic to the health fund next door to the buddhists to pay my dues is it a
lotus or a zimmer frame that i ought to consider or just new fabric for the friday
night lounge spooks & murphy lotsa death certs but how sweet the sleep after
though not the snore

frame

so what was yesterday   a journey through
the land of carpet with a sulky vacuum cleaner
nothing new in the swirls of lost hair crumbs and
missing peas no divining in the beige down there,
i skim across the illustrated pages of 'the gods
of freud' that full wing of eros is worth searching
for; i have settled for my own framed postcard of
tyche, a daughter of zeus, the goddess of chance &
guardian of place, the walls of the small city she wears
on her head let in plenty of light through their curved
apertures i hail her with my deodorant torch called exotic
spice and my crimson towel unfurled from my head,
i'm an untidy town   oh save me –

verb

your book of dreams: it always fails
the exam, why not think of yourself
as an ambulance, then there will be
no need to dial triple O, telephones
become more difficult to find these days,
such little things obscured in domestic
mess; so follow that beam of light in the tunnel
any sort of breath will pay the toll, just what part
of the verb are you seeking, the journey is
shorter than you

choir

i turn my head it rattles like a world
that's lost its spin in allergies, a choir
of off-tune scribbled chores
                    could it list towards
elysium if   a wind were fierce, benign enough
                    yeah   blow winds blow, time edges
                         forwards to five o'clock

*

program the brain for bank-alert   snap crackle pop
   600 dollars in   600 out   nods the smiling
      teller still bright at 5 minutes to 5   into the shabby
                 wallet i shove the 600 –

an irritated mother investing for her
   2 year old in a term deposit   monies from
godma 'n' grandpa   and assorted other lovers   cannot
      understand why the bank won't issue a mini-book:
   an official donor history –
                 i'd like to say   dear   why not try
   a diy a notebook from myer or dj-s   blueboyblue
         you can draw up a table   and he'll soon
   be able   to title-page it in non-toxic texta   but the
         indignant sway of her pony tail keeps me

away i'd better
leave with some mental credit

*

the steamed
dim sims taste intelligent delicious i survey
tiers of iced broccoli in the
farm-fresh garden
on the first floor
of a professional
tower
my gastroenterologist don't live here
anymore
and neither does ballard from
shepparton, uk with his vision
curtains lighting the way

to impulse pp-pamper my head
i pick up an 'elegance' hair
accessory kit exclusive! at the ground floor
aldi store i'll take a long
black with nietzsche the germans
always give good head
so where's that 9 grain goethebread

channel

i had a dream   of rose gardens
but the power lines were too tied up
in old conversations to respond –
still small memory worms curled through
the trip   station after station   where 'sons and lovers'
had once rested on my lap
while i juggled with a bitter coffee
or the sting of a salt and vinegar
breakfast of freshly crinkled cuts

once the terror of a hopkins' sonnet had been
assuaged by the green whooshing of market
gardens   through the stiff windows   now the glare of mortgaged
skies grown fat with high rise craving   is shooting at the
breeze   no one's at home on the balconies   not
even the view of the view

***

inside the destination there were to be surprises
the memorial park with its memorial
cannon   and the squalking of a thousand white
cockatoos
– a consolation prize?

[&   the hospital bed art in the plaza tilted
like bed pans on strike]

but the video aprons were beautiful, one for every week
of a year, fabric after fabric displayed as if part
of a valuable diary   it was time to channel
betty king   or crocker
and prepare for that dinner party with a
liquid diet [i've forgotten its name]   so i
could wear that silvery
apron   made from such delicate
'kerchiefs it moved
like angels' breath

– was it time   for a musical   i discovered a
hard sausage roll

***

perry como & betty grable sang
in the op shop i was kissed
by the lips of luck
there on the sturdy whatnot [not wicker]
in miscellanea's preloved midst
was a fine glass egg cup   my fifty cent
placebo or saviour   looking out for a
falling star or a pocket   or
a fresh little paper rose

trunk

through the narrow window
[at first i wrote 'widow']
of the art gallery, right next to kiefer's *palmsonntag*
you can see its masts   a conversation
of fresh flags in the long winter wind
a ship from chile
docked in woolloomooloo bay for a week   green and white
against the grey of our warships   it's the *esmeralda* folks
i don't know
why it's here but i do know   where it's beeeen
one of
pinochet's torture ships [he must have had more than one]
that voyaged over waters beyond
the radar of the scream
the long trunk of the dead giant palm tree on the floor
of the gallery absorbs my nausea
some thing has lain down its life
even in death its roots are startling
and the herringbone
fern that shoots out from near
its crown is green more green
than *esmeralda*   ode   threnode   this morning
i pull my 33 year old copy of neruda
off the dusty shelf *estante polvo*   and turn to 'oda al tomate'
where the assassinated tomatoes become stars
of the earth in less than 2 pages *el tomate astro de tierra*

the bus took me home more
quickly than i had expected the roads were dry
   and watchful   the painted coffee table fills with worms
      the arm chair grows new fabric   the earth
         still darker than the shiver of night, and the fridge has
                                                    frozen the salad

road

sibylance

sun sings through the dust of the window
and the silver sink what a birdshine, lime
rind glows through the jam jar, epiphany
way above the trench of garbage bins down
below, you could be fishing on any old river
right now this could be one of your last finer split
second moments, meet me on the golden green;
there is movement in the grimy courtyard someone
shifting apartments dumping decor, a framed photo
of marilyn maybe madonna maybe not, more likely
a poster of a georgia o'keefe bloom, jaded floral art
a little crinkled where a vodkatini or an orgasm hit the wall:
moma moma where art thou; past the front door packs
of paris hilton wannabes looking likely in sunfrocks
skim along the streets towards skinny lattes, all eyes
preying for someone to snap them inside a slow
myth at the crossroads

road

i have nothing exciting to tell
you mostly they were friendly but some
people looked through me the juice
of the lime is no longer fresh i have never
before seen myself as a window when the bus
travels this road i always sigh i am surprised by
my new interest in apples especially pink
ladies peak hour is not like other peaks i am tired
of people who work in shops saying of my partner how
is your sister patience is not a prominent feature of
my fingernails false smoke alarms have replaced
church bells clumps of tissues squat on the floor like chooks
demanding to be fed those toes could feature in a hitchcock
movie the paragraph has become a doormat i was not
paid to broadcast this i slept through space odyssey 2001 of
course you remind me of someone anyone with windy
eyes would do

fridge magnet

the recorded opera rising like schnitzelling nostalgia
all conversation sweats across the mousse, ibis squat
on backpacks in the postcard riddled park

archbishops sip cool beers on subliminal rooftops
police parade in six packs spraying cracks in the
paving: show us your passport kiddo you don't smell

australian; the hospital seemed like a palace until
you're forced to buy back your own blood served
in ice cubes; elbows need translating this january afternoon

plank

they were indignant with the
gossip that they all wrote
the same way not a pdf dissident
among them   are you a photocopy
or a plagiarist   a clone or a row of
paper dolls   how blonde is your
keyboard

they disappeared through
the small canyon between the
octave and the sestet
scanning their breaths for the latest
therapy the barcode just
a few metres from their fugitive
feet

wharf song

the floor stretches   amplifies   as the poets
read to the microphone proud for a moment
like the prototype of a linoleum polish
and or the beginning of a pindaric ode
– could a continent locate a small
ripple in its mind depressed deep
beneath a rock economy; fresh impatience
chucks a prickly bouquet from the mirrors
of its dance studio and poetry slinks
back into the darkness of pockets, as a
saw pokes its teeth through the partition
the generic wine flooding the loss of words
like a late transfusion

extract

the distraction sieve
the remainder
a reminder

*

the last marble
pluralised
write a note
to lord elgin
where is that
block of
memo cube
refills 500
sheets

*

mis muebles
today i must
dust mis muebles

*

it's easy she said
just flick and tick

*

i long to measure
the final curtains
the tape coils
like a coy snake
mas o menos

*

mis cortinas
drive for all
your worth

hunch

how many sandy creeks can
a language bear they were so hard
to identify through a wind pipe,
the cream for the devonshire tea defiant
as a brick you couldn't see the two tree
hill behind the red jumbo; so what is the point
of disappointment this was a world of sheds: sales
and erections – and wet dreams aquariums; people
were falling above our four bedroom car – the valley
spread below in laconic grandeur : quibbles
vanished into the view the air wore your hunched
feet into waffles; return that insurance guide

hostess

rain shone through the
sunlight like a boutique theory
of redemption; we kicked
up our heels ready for the gypsy
tap or a gentle polka; someone
heard portia gift wrapping castanets
with a chop munching priest   so was
the casket of steroids an entertainment
device to motivate a jury like a bowl
of minties   as the parachutes blew
open it was anybody's guess –

hoop

the day lurched in funerals
sorrow dampened the lawns
like abandoned teacups, carparks
whined with impatient ghosts who
wanted to get the legalities on the
table before the fireplaces turned
cold; but the fresh ballgowns
hanging in the historic coach
house were a reminder memory's
cheek is warm

sesame

the flowers on the cactus
came and went like
a speed boat across the plate
glass   you wake up and then you
fall asleep wink quick or is it
the reverse; everything so fast
you can't remember when you last
saw the wallet for the war ration
coupons it smelt a little mouldy
the last time you found it unsure
of how to access its navy blue
emptiness   a thought vanishes
into the air's crevices you have to
rely on your fingers for good tips
a beachcomber's manual will not
help, you knew how to reach for
the wall when the salt water stung
your eyes   [maybe] the best thing
to do between the tick and the tock
is to hold your breath: the air's veins
open like a patient map you won't
need a good vocabulary

impedimenta

more calories were burnt
than you could poke a chip
at packing a few items into
a notebook the detective rose
like a bicycle a poem is a
dead thing was his large print
conclusion the clubhouse dug
deep into the corporate scrapcraft
for a totem a familial celebration
remote as any imagination itching for
an escape route through the vat

tick

last drinks at the
friendship bar evanescence
is my pashmina no apology
for the lack of a biography
anyone could see it
coming runes in the fettuccini
is one way of looking at it i
suppose all the decades of
romping in the hay production
figures never disputed now it's
time to leave the wagon to
serenade its own wheels   how
black the glossy stars this enchanted
evening mario stranger than anything you
could call terrestrial bow ties

dry mouth

dazed tribunes
ankle deep in the gutters
of wasted candidates   faces
and numbers smiling elect me
me me me, o paper democracy

toxin cocktails pour
through the streets the
beauty parlours fill with
shickered youth, bukowski
is in town

batwing spring rolls in
the mall, the tiber bar
banking on a flood of
lucre, policy fatigue propels
a dry mouth into liquor
factions   generations
screech like tattooed
cockatoos

                    penthouses
look down with vain derision
sipping virgin breast milk on
the rocks   retinal recognition

elevators temporarily out of
action a gang of ballardeers
rides the stairs with hungry
passwords

who twangs a bluegrass of regret

breath

do you hold a licence
to hum that old ballad
from last year's hit list
in the street   if you blow
your nose your registration
number will let you know,
the body such an appliance
even if you slump on the chemist's
step like a heritage   with a bunch
of cheap chocolates from the $1 shop
up your sleeve honey ripe cherry comb
you can enjoy a little sweetness trickling
down your chin's resignation   the beep
of another overdose insists it's alive   such
a bargain   come on down

string

we had forgotten
how to turn the page
the yawn salad didn't
include an instruction
manual, and the
columbines at the matinee
broke all molar resolutions
a betadine cocktail was
no real answer as the trivia
quizz broke into a riot
when some body argued that
shakespeare had ghost written
'the sentimental bloke'; it was
hard to keep any of the eggs
in baskets let alone the one –

please circulate the wrigleys
but avoid an irritable jaw
it is perhaps better to dance
like supper till the gene
pool opens: you can then
whet an appetite for the price
of a towel

sigh

devout as narcissism
insincere as litanies of
the mumble hours
clumps from a tonsure
session feather the parquetry
tiles: fringes of hair around
bare skulls, circular pathways
to gardens of shrivelled delights;
is a curia eleison a substitute
for savlon – gossip's tonsils
sure of something on the couch
of sighs, an amphora of iced nero
fetched from the eastern wing;
craniums to be polished till they
shine like a procession   is this what
the butler saw –

lark

prod the long word
that flirts and jiggles in the goggles
a portal to a distant epilogue

and then the elastic rain falls down
imagination's fiesty soda
voyager on the rum

what star slurps reclining
in the empyrean's outpost
ogling fiction's lullaby

test tube hallucination or
peripatetic eidolon

ersatz avatar chomps on next
millennium's poppy harvest
uber daddy's paying for pranks

teflon icarus dogpaddling
home for more –

matchbox semaphore

tick off those stale occasions
data on a clipboard and discard –
conceal the megaphone in the loft

can a day ever be named
anything other than this
patch of portable air

any wristwatch betrays the
expectation   better yield
to the fresh glitch of just
being here avoiding that
eyebrow quiz   do you
need stationery for that

squander

the tv won't desist from announcing
it's smart the bored fireworks long
for redundancy packages sushis unroll
across city food courts like yogic
rebellions emporial merchants dice
the language with viral cupid-ity
too many carrots can't locate enough
jaws monthly plans seem far too
abstemious receipts piling up like karmic
deliriums architectures goad the skies
with aphasic cranes pop up fur salons coup
in all the best plazas feet itch by the million
so many things that bite through the night

cheap

twisting in polyethylene spheralities
i interact with galaxy clusters
i was a freelance bride last week

i remember how i had been a cowgirl
when i nourished a family root

i became an organic present
like a true workshop leader
i have worn website shoes to work

i found my hands in the prairie show
i have more dignity than clothes

i have thought about poetry as hypertension
as i write these recipes for first aid and scholarship

i am easy to sing

could i moonlight as a sub committee
it's all vaudeville

it grows on you

you lift a hand to sweep away
the cobwebs   a rubber spider
is about to infiltrate your best
eye   so entertain it with sweet
valentines   the people in the park
may still be there even if you
dare not think of them or understand
their costume jewelry

the medieval greyhound flares across
your passage like a literal confirmation
can you read the subtext of that
syringe dangling at the periphery
of the paper rose

do you like the digitally enhanced
duck pond of the sesquicentenary
parklands   tick all the boxes as
your lapdog poos in paradise clearly
please

is this where the national lector
slept with her tattered script,
a dream of playing tennis on
a painted lawn with hamlet;

how the rows of trams burned
brighter than ilium or carthage
i saw the exhibition – some inferno
and then i hit the sack

delivery

delivery

i.

delve your soft nose
inside the couch grass
as if there's an answer
or just something spectacular
beneath, beyond the wiles of
pluto; the grey limbs of the frangipani
tree might squint your eyesight if you try
to read them too closely & the wind's library
full of sandy salt operas and skeltering portents

ii.

my name tumbled down the hill so often as *you*
called me to set the table i seek *your* voice in a
notional warmth, these tissues of nostalgia; i delivered
the gossip of the streets swift from the corner store:
sitting on bags of dark potatoes with a sharpened ear
while waiting to buy the cigarettes and cheddar, those
chthonic smells of the hessian sackcloth; the boredom
of taking the dolls to the beach down the driveway, you
could only pretend to be a child so many times –

a later page

[not quite after Elizabeth Bishop's 'In the Waiting Room']

i didn't have an existential moment
[epiphanic?] at the dentist in my childhood
– unlike elizabeth bishop when she examined
the *national geographic* in a waiting room
in wartime worcester massachusetts,
february 1918 – while her aunt was in
'the chair'; a visit to the dentist in sydney
town, corner pitt & market, was almost
entertainment – 'he' was only uncle bob,
virtual in-law, whose laugh and haircut
evoked bob hope for me; i didn't mind
the climb up to the chair in the creamy
surgery with its enamel gloss that sheen
of instruments in rows a floor or so above
the benign world of *shirley shoes*, the city
gleamed just outside the window while
he might probe and prod; it was the cold
war years but my seven year old veins were
warm with scents of post-appointment pleasure:
a restaurant visit, tour of bright department stores,
a trip to the arcane library, its rich, urgent papersmell,
the return journey boarded from a tram circling [like gold]
queen victoria's statue at queens square

there was the *saturday evening post* and maybe
the new yorker in the modest waiting room, nothing
to alarm me – or perhaps the wait was pretty short
at uncle bob's; instead a copy of *the saturday book*
belonging to my parents became the rite of passage,
realisation for me: sick in bed i trawled through it
gazing at the pics – a secret strobe of joy viewing can-can
dancers kicking up their legs   then   that sudden endless
moment on a later page: a group of people at the races,
    edwardian
i think, laughing laughing at the camera but i believed entirely
that they laughed at me   weak and maybe measly in my mother's
bed   no asylum underneath the sheets, that arabian tent illusion
had outgrown its glamour at least a year before

a mercurial terror i would jolt into
on reaching *love locked out* while
browsing an old book of national gallery
illustrations 1926 never lasted long
[the backview of a naked boy outside
a heavy metal door like a frozen metaphor]

but those sharp eyes and mouths of racy laughter
bouncing off the walls dismissive and derisive
drill through collapsing years

comb

i.

bondi was always as big as
tomorrow, or something wider
more thrilling than time –
something huge that could reach
out and lift you, once you swam
through and over the waves or dived
under to grab at the challenge of sand
avoiding the careless/careful will of a
dumper; it was big enough for everyone
to think it was theirs

ii.

even the sewer outlet water, its stream
etched into the beach right down to the surf,
could not stain bondi's ascendency; nor could
a poem 'ode to depravity' composed by a fifteen
year old student of shelley, looking down on
the scene from the top deck of a bus roaring
onto campbell parade in the gloom of a wintery
gale: the ocean the beach the sky all so grey

and remember
the stories of rats in the old wooden dressing sheds
at the ocean view baths where the waves crashed

over the side, defying the odds of a champion swim;
those ladies' swimming club pennants and badges
may rot in a shoebox or lavender trunk – but waves
never retire

iii.

not as spiritually glamorous as balmoral, another 'b'
beach – with young krishnamurti avatar saviour almost
paramahansa sailing resplendent into its shore; no uplifter
of souls but of 'public' standards was mister aub laidlaw,
bondi beach king, judge of what kind of flesh could be
revealed on his shore [his aubrahamaniac bikini law];
whose white zinc lipped cohorts tried to remove and
charge a visiting german hair care company executive
changing out of his bathers inside a handsome beach robe
of black on the shore, while the chrism of suntan oil from
the on the beach kiosk sprayed quotidian radiance
over the bodies in the heliophile queue

iv.

boyfriends boyfriends twisting rocking
the summers away; bondi a map of significant
fickle and frivolous moments; here and here
here and there: forgotten names faceless
renewable eidetic: promenade pavilion sandbank
smooth waves: mash of lipstick and hairspray

pashing in holdens above ben buckler's danish
mermaids: hips swinging easily naively –
the 'peppermint twist' at the pink 'orcades'

v.

snooze-drifts on a towel with its appliqued
pocket of secrets, wave echoes fizz and
froth down through your ears – you could
stay there forever, your book 'ides of march',
an epistolary novel by thornton wilder, about
caesar's rome, is splayed flat, spine almost
melting, underneath the sprawl of
a surrendering knee you have been seduced
and suitably salted this glistering empire
of ocean and sand

grip

time rolls down the tolerant
hill from the secular bus stop

you can wax your feet with a
candle stub and join up for the ride –

lie on the road as it turns
the corner just for the heck of it

the whiff of warm tar makes a day
less boring in a long hot summer when

temperance jigs on the porch like a
rampant djinn: anxiety seeping through

that unwrapped gift of the iliad, you suck
on the toffee or fate sucks on you

bury the long necks under the hibiscus
and hear a modest future bloom;

the beat of the tennis ball against
the high garage wall can improve

a backhand and volley the charm
of elastic hooked to the ball like a

hero no smashing of window glass
at the kitchen sink; you'll sit

like a sunset, tuck into a soft
chop and two tone salad minus

the orange ring the accusation of ocean
smothered in the folds of a frayed epaulette

harbinger

i.

siliconed stacks of glass
reflect the harbour
miracle of gliding windows
multiplying the view an
extended prologue
to an opaque parable

this is my postcard city
my teatowel my snowdome
my archival ferry ticket, my
effusive chalice point of
view point my malaise
yes my swamp of leisure –
how a cruise ship, 'liner'
tracy says, slides through
your waters like a
trojan horse

ii.

why was a japanese light plane
able to complete its reconnaissance
mission flying in and out of sydney
harbour right up to the bridge and
not be intercepted, in 1942; urban
legend where is your tee-shirt

iii.

this is where flying boats
departed and arrived to
and from 'the islands', the rose
bay flying boat base, hear
them purr across easy fronds
of post war summer waters,
frangipani suitcases of new
pacific dreams; i'm happy
sucking jaffas on the slap up
steps of the nearby rsl; jason
and the argonauts were never
moored near my palm tree

iv.

sit on the seat outside
elizabeth bay house imagine
the historic gardens of alexander
and elizabeth mcleay rolling
down towards the harbour 'a sylvan
coup d'oeil' said the sydney gazette,
'a little paradise' nodded dr. george
bennett; 'a few english showers would
improve it' wrote georgiana lowe

my eyes reach over to the bay
around to darling point and

the hills above the heads, and so
continues lowe 'the bays are
innumerable, and resemble the scotch
salt-water lochs'; this area of sydney
around what is now nicknamed betty
bay was once known as blacktown,
macquarie having had it reserved [that
is 'put aside'] for the aborigines

v.

just hours before he died
i took his pocket radio and
earphones, that he would use at
the cricket, to the sea wall at rose bay
and sat on the ledge behind the shops,
just along from the demolished
wintergarden theatre where we'd seen
so many movies, stories rising from
the harbour on a velvet screen; and
i noted a small ferry crossing
the entrance to the bay; 'mad about
you' was playing loudly in my head, a
gust of windsurfers moving suddenly
into view

from 'crevice' a mnemonica

i. no doubt about it

i read doris lessing in delphi
short stories on the oregano trail –
then the bronze charioteer asked
me out for dinner, i forgot to say
no; at chandigarh i drank
six bottles of limca as a man
breathed under sand near the
bus station for a rupee, a town
where the bank ran out of money
for thirty minutes then i bought
'coolie' to read under my room
fan the postcards vanished
into the wall; i noticed god
hastening down the hill
by the river at rishikesh afraid
of being recognised –
i wore time like a birthday
there was no one to tell me
what to do –

ii. chorus

a morning of false
fiancées, you fluked
a pose till the salad

dazzled like a coup;
the celebration at
epidaurus, sunset
medea; the guards
in white hats circled
the horde of stones,
suspicious of anything
restless in the air –
it was raucous awe
and postcards by midnight
you were all as young
as those rusty odes

iii. soaked

the well, full of gossip and
whisper, myths got confused
in the hangovers everyone had
nicknames it was our map to
the lore, a dramatis personae
for the cognac sippers in
the siesta we played
their role in our awkward
holiday like gauche puppets,
the empty barn a dark treasury
for what could not be named;
joyce's ulysses got soaked in
red wine the waves broke in

a hard currency on the shore –
the wooden slats saved our feet
from a hot sand's intolerance we
took the bargain option of slipping into
the murky lagoon; the relique windmill
way above the ocean was our talisman
and obrigad how we flew –

iv. plinth

a boat eating a rock's history
too much sun in your diary
things scar your pockets like
awkward souvenirs; the hand
me down visa fades into another
century the secret of the retsina
rotting old photographs   still here
with a donkey load of memories you
don't know what to do with, the more
prepositions you manufacture the more you
encourage them like a clamour of bees

v. kidney

the belly replied to
the sea food like a diva
a new music swayed in
the lemon grass – sheets crackled

and smelt as they should in a
velvet hotel the key napped
in its pearly shell: you
could hardly believe this
invocation; a private swim
in a private pool, kidney
shaped intimacy a tropical
garland of neon plants
and the dust of delhi dispersed

a travel magazine is redundant
research – pineapple princess breezes
through the foyer to the aqua tour
bus, james bond island stunned
like a camera: the tick of
buddha thought in the third
dark cave amplified those days –

wooing the owl

(or the great sleep forward)

rest

the room so silent it grows full
with presence a myth surprises with
its resilience it's as if you slumber
in a soft bread basket your eyelids
sealed lightly in compliance; a dark expansion,
an atmosphere: you know that she is here and
there: above behind around you the owl you know
but cannot always see, she rests on the light bowl's
citadel, one eye missing, a fugitive to archaeology,
the other swift and clear and kind as intuition, imperial as time

punctual

an almost word of the early
hours some thing green about
it ~ did it waft in from a health
brochure there was a paragraph
and then this word i kept trying to
remember it, something shonky
in its grammatical context i was
falling deeper asleep over and
over   should a dream be harassed
by rules or memory   a barking dog
shook off the dingy harbour water
as it leapt to the punctual shore

nightclubbing

oneiric reproductions
tired old dreams you have tried to dump them
in the refuse bins but your molecular nostalgic
nature snaps them back and you are re-possessed:
    a forest of rogue documents harangues within your temple
    this sadistic bureaucracy of images and words even the chutzpah
    of your snores can't punch them through the walls

frontier

the happy occasion of the
popcorn doona: you can make
the film or star in it or both, the cup
of camomile glowing under the night lamp
like a wishing well as you snuggle down
into your festival of big surprises, you multi-
locational polymorph, and the popcorn swells
above you like golden fleece; at the scratch of dawn
you may wake feeling crook, but the shepherd's out
stripping the corn

buzz

you sleep in a tinge of postmortem green
is there enough memory download remaining
to lipsync *o my charona*   the camera
you swallowed is not tax deductible
and is non operable, but you glimpse your last
organs there on the jumble sale table, you implore
the salt shaker to give you a break – you need that
wake up call like you need a caesura; at this point
two jehovah's witnesses, one at a time, buzz on the intercom,
polite as all get out, keen to alert you to the usual
apocalypse

how authentic

how you got there you don't
know but you had your ticket –
the queue was long and punctuated
by a scatter of discarded garments,
a serenade of gutted candles reinforced
some frail tradition   the ticket was torn
and nameless but it felt right in your hand:
someone will know you by the way you
stand

prang

a morris minor somersaults over
an inclining rock garden, a keen
law student slurps brandy from a
tumbler deckled with rolling dice,
darkness was cerebral so was
the bloody ambulance
                                        the holiday avenue
paved with tennis courts and candy
striped rumpus rooms   pillars of
society eschewing culpability   breakfast
on the terrace with cubes of sugared
grapefruit and transfusions of tomato
juice, stock reports fornicate with glossy
magazines   speed driving with body
parts just another prang   the icecream
cake splendid in the frigidaire

armistice

you take a detour through
the tinge of mountains
a miniature train toots
like a rehearsed homecoming
before an interlude of sand
storms and their random
love letters; when you
arrive at a front porch
a man in an aggravated
suit sleeps like a ransacked
brewery in the spokes
of first light a paperback copy
of a dale carnegie manual dents
a felt hat's crown aster daisies
in a yellow front door vase decline
to supervise

                    where to now old
psyche   is this methodism on the cusp
of a bootlace surprise   the mattress
protection cover resists any further surmise

nurse

no commemorative plate
the dream
can you find its co-ordinates
no compass, or protractor
will it return for a showy
visit like an american fleet
a dream cloth offered
like the turin shroud
did i mean to say cloud
somewhere in the ghost kibbutz
you could just hear *hava nagila*
a blue card an embossed
gold crown inside a cheque
with an amount to fill in what
job is to be completed a nurse
removes the silver cage of emergency
medicine next to the bed in the
no name hospital the banana
lounge hung round for ages like
a document are the palestinians
coming home

the great sleep forward

to think like a pond
or a puddle

ponder this how many
sleeps till death

is your face a lake
veronica after

the night mask
visitation

the instruction beeped
talking while sleeping
strictly prohibited

snuggle down in your
percale qualms

mosey along those
synapses as if in
the ponderosa, no
snorting please or
you could be cactus

even if the eucalyptus oil
smudge disambulates the
huntsman spider

disambiguate here now

vaginas are sleeping like
there's no tomorrow

organically challenging wha –

snowy

they flash past
like cyclists through
red lights with or without
consequence   is there a need
to hurry   is there an agenda
as they wait for particle
rearrangement, reassignment
another incarnation; do they
get impatient or is this messing
around merely spirit at play, a
version of 'being' italicised; are
the dead on the look out for
groceries, hungry as they visit
dreams footpaths crevices
vestibules auditory canals, beings
we recognise, or don't; what
fills the space between the 'be'
and the 'ing', what would coleridge
have to say in his lime-tree bower;
you surprised me deep in slumber
under the snowy doona, your
emerald dress like a sudden
summer –

frill

for loma

at last the stitches in time's
pesky little roster break it's
a chronologically free for
all you're everywhere at once
though your feet are motionless
asleep that's the only way to move your
frilly heart grows bigger than a cabbage
hear it whistle in the pillow's dune